THE PERFORMANCE
OF
BECOMING HUMAN

Feb 2017

THE PERFORMANCE
OF
BECOMING HUMAN

Daniel Borzutzky

Brooklyn Arts Press | New York

The Performance of Becoming Human
© 2016 Daniel Borzutzky

ISBN-13: 978-1-936767-46-5

Cover design by Joe Pan. Interior design by Lynne DeSilva-Johnson.
Edited by Broc Rossell.

Published in the United States of America by:
Brooklyn Arts Press
154 N 9th St #1
Brooklyn, NY 11249
WWW.BROOKLYNARTSPRESS.COM
INFO@BROOKLYNARTSPRESS.COM

Distributed to the trade by Small Press Distribution / SPD
www.spdbooks.org

Library of Congress Cataloging-in-Publication Data

Names: Borzutzky, Daniel.
Title: The performance of becoming human / Daniel Borzutzky.
Description: Brooklyn, NY : Brooklyn Arts Press, [2016]
Identifiers: LCCN 2015028529 | ISBN 9781936767465 (pbk. : alk. paper)
Classification: LCC PS3602.O79 A6 2016 | DDC 811/.6--dc23
LC record available at http://lccn.loc.gov/2015028529

SIXTH PRINTING

MIX
Paper from
responsible sources
FSC® C011935

Acknowledgments

Thanks to the editors of the following journals and anthologies for publishing some of these poems: *American Poets in the 21st Century: Global Poetics*; *Angels of the Americlypse: New Latin@ Writing*; *Boston Review*; *Devouring the Green: The Cyborg Lyric Anthology {Poetry in an Era of Catastrophic Change}*; *Jai Alai*; *jubilat*; *Mandorla: New Writing from the Americas*; *Matter: A Journal of Political Poetry and Commentary*; *PEN Poetry Series*; *Petra*; *Sprung Formal*; and *Your Impossible Voice*.

Some of these poems were published in the chapbook *Bedtime Stories for the End of the World!* (Bloof Books, 2014) and others in *Memories of my Overdevelopment* (Kenning Editions, 2015).

CONTENTS

THE PERFORMANCE
OF
BECOMING HUMAN

LET LIGHT SHINE OUT OF DARKNESS

I live in a body that does not have enough light in it

For years, I did not know that I needed to have more light

Once, I walked around my city on a dying morning and a decomposing body approached me and asked me why I had no light

I knew this decomposing body

All that remained of it were teeth, bits of bone, a hand

It came to me and said: There is no light that comes out of your body

I did not know at the time that there should have been light in my body

It's not that I am dead

It's not that I am translucent

It's that you cannot know you need something if you do not know it is missing

Which is not to say that for years I did not ask for this light

Once, I even said to the body I live with: I think I need more light in my body, but I really did not take this seriously as a need, as something I deserved to have

I said: I think I need for something blue or green to shine from my rib cage

Other times when I am talking about lightness I am talking about breath and space and movement

For it is hard to move in a body so congested with images of mutilation

Did you hear the one about the illegal immigrant who electrocuted his employee's genitals? Did you hear the one about the boy in Chicago whose ear was bitten off when he crossed a border he did not know existed?

I want to give you more room to move so I am trying to carve a space, with light, for you to walk a bit more freely

This goes against my instincts, which are to tie you down, to tie you to me, to bind us by the wrist the belly the neck and to look directly into your mouth, to make you open your mouth and speak the vocabulary of obliteration right into your tongue your veins your blood

I stop on a bridge over the train tracks and consider the history of the chemical-melting of my skin

Once, when I poured a certain type of acid on my arm I swore I saw a bright yellow gas seep out of my body

Once, my teeth glowed sick from the diseased snow they had shoved into my mouth when they wanted me to taste for myself, to bring into my body the sorrows of the rotten carcass economy

Once, I dreamwrote that I found my own remains in a desert that was partially in Chile and partially in Arizona

Was I a disappeared body, tossed out of an airplane by a bureaucrat-soldier-compatriot or was I a migrant body who died from dehydration while crossing the invisible line between one civilization and another

I was part of a team of explorers   we were searching for our own bodies

In the desert I found my feet and I put them in a plastic bag and photographed them, cataloged them, weighed and measured them and when I was finished with the bureaucratization of my remains I lay down in the sand and asked one of my colleagues to jam a knife into my belly

She obliged

But when the blade entered my skin it was as if my belly were a water balloon

Water shot into the air

My skin ripped into hundreds of pieces and I watched as the water covered the feet of my colleagues who were here to document their disappearances and decomposition

It was at this moment that I saw light in my body   not sun over the sand but a drip of soft blue on a piece of skin that had fallen off my body and dissolved into its own resistance

THE PERFORMANCE OF BECOMING HUMAN

On the side of the highway a thousand refugees step off a school bus and into a sun that can only be described as "blazing."

The rabbi points to the line the refugees step over and says: "That's where the country begins."

This reminds me of Uncle Antonio. He would have died had his tortured body not been traded to another country for minerals.

Made that up.

This is a story about diplomatic protections.

The refugees were processed through Austria or Germany or maybe Switzerland.

Somehow they were discovered in some shit village in some shit country by European soldiers and taken to an embassy where they were promptly bathed, injected with vaccines, interrogated, etc.

Their bodies were traded by country A in exchange for some valuable natural resource needed by country B.

There was only one gag, says the rabbi, as he tucks his children into bed. So the soldiers took turns passing the filthy thing back and forth between the mouths of the two prisoners. The mother and son licked each other's slobber off the dirty rag that had been in who knows how many other mouths.

You love to write about this, don't you?

I am paid by the word for my transcriptions. Just one more question about the gag.

He wants to know what color the gag was, what it was made of, how many mouths had licked it. Hundreds, thousands, tens of thousands?

They used their belts to bind them by the waist to the small cage they were trapped in.

Everything reminds me of a story about an ape captured on a boat by a group of European soldiers who showed him how to become human by teaching him how to spit and belch.

Everything is always about the performance of becoming human.

Observing a newly processed refugee, the rabbi says: "I have seen those blue jeans before."

At times like this, he thinks: I can say just about anything right now.

This is, after all, a bedtime story for the end of the world.

I am moving beneath the ground and not sleeping and trying to cross the border from one sick part of the world to another.

But where is the light and why does it not come in through your bloody fingers?

You hold your bloody fingers before my eyes and there is light in them but I cannot see it.

You say: There are countries in my bloody fingers. I am interested in the borders.

Or: I am interested in the gas chambers in your collapsible little fingers.

You put them to my face and I see your hands open and in them I see a thick wall and a sky and an ocean and ten years pass and it is still nighttime and I am falling and there are bodies on the ground in your bloody hands.

Think about the problem really hard then let it go and when you least expect it a great solution will appear in your mind.

The broken bodies stand by the river and wait for the radiation to trickle out of the houses and into their skin.

They stand under billboards and sniff paint and they know the eyes that watch them own their bodies.

A more generous interpretation might be that their bodies are shared between the earth, the state and the bank.

The sentences are collapsing one by one and the bodies are collapsing in your bloody hands and you stitch me up and pray I will sleep and you tell me of the shattered bus stops where the refugees are waiting for the buses to take them to the mall where they are holding us now and there is a man outside our bodies making comments about perspective and scale and light and there is light once more in your bloody fingers.

All I see is the sea and my mother and father falling into it.

Again? That's like the most boring image ever.

The water is frozen and we are sleeping on the rocks, watching the cows on the cliff and you tell me they might fall and break open and that sheep and humans and countries will fall out of them and that this will be the start of the bedtime story you will tell me on this our very last night on earth.

Come closer, you say, with your eyes.

Move your bloody face next to mine and rub me with it. We are dying from so many stories. We are not complete in the mind from so many stories of burning houses, missing children, slaughtered animals. Who will put the stories back together and who will restore the bodies? I am working towards the end but first I need a stab, a small slice. The stories they are there but we need a bit more wit. We need something lighter to get us to the end of this story. Did you hear the one about the guy who picked up chicks by quoting the oral testimonies of the illiterate villagers who watched their brothers and sisters get slaughtered?

Or:

Andalé andalé arriba arriba welcome to Tijuana you cannot eat anymore barbecued iguana.

Have you met Speedy Gonzales' cousin?

His name is Slow Poke Rodrigues.

En español se llama Lento Rodrigues.

He's a drunk little fucking mouse.

His predator, the lazy cat baking in the sun, thinks he will taste good with chili peppers but there's something I forgot to tell you. Slow Poke always pack a gun and now he's going to blow your flabbergasted feline face off.

It was 1987 and my friends from junior high trapped me on the floor and mashed bananas in my face and sang: It's no fun being an illegal alien!

You know you can die from so many stories.

The puddy cat guards the AJAX cheese factory behind the fence, right across the border.

The wetback mice see the gringo cheese.

They smell the gringo cheese.

Your gringo cheese it smells so good.

They need Speedy Gonzales to get them some ripe, fresh, stinky gringo cheese.

Do you know this Speedy Gonzales, asks one of the starving wetback mice.

I know him, Speedy Gonzales frens with my seester (the mice laugh). Speedy Gonzales frens with everybody's seester.

Ha ha ha the little border-crossing, sneak-fucking mouses think it's cute that they're invading our culture to steal our cheese but it don't make a difference because you and I (cue the rhythm and blues) we are taking a stroll on the electrified fence of love cause I feel a little Southern Californian transnational romance coming on right about now.

I feel like Daniel from the Karate Kid because I too once had a Southern Californian experience where I wasn't aware I was learning ancient Japanese secrets when I was waxing on and waxing off.

And I am with you Mr. Miyagi in Reseda.

I am with you Mr. Miyagi in Pasadena.

And I am with you Mr. Miyagi at the All Valley Karate tournament.

And I am with you Mr. Miyagi in Okinawa where you went in Karate Kid II to meet your long lost girlfriend when you discovered she wasn't married off when she was just a teenager to your fiercest Okinawan rival.

And I am with you Mr. Miyagi in Tijuana where it's murder and diarrhea and always kinda kinky.

But seriously, friends:

What *do* you make of this darkness that surrounds us?

They chopped up two dozen bodies last night and today I have to pick up my dry cleaning.

In the morning I need to assess student learning outcomes as part of an important administrative initiative to secure the nation's future by providing degrees of economic value to the alienated, urban youth.

So for now hasta luego compadres and don't worry too much about the bucket of murmuring shit that is the unitedstatesian night.

What does it say? What does it say? What do you want it to say?

IN THE BLAZING CITIES OF YOUR ROTTEN CARCASS MOUTH

Too bad we live in a world so uptight that we can't have things like the Frito Bandito anymore.

-Comment on YouTube

The children were eating the bushes outside of their former houses that had been crushed by The Bank of America.

There was a boy in a bush singing an improvised song about a bulldozer that obliterates the bureaucratic centers of the earth.

Do you remember cheese, he sang to his friend.

Te acuerdas de la piña?

Do you remember ferries, he sang.

Te acuerdas de los patos?

Do you remember school bells and cowards and the boys who would come to our yard to eat the scraps of food we threw to them before the city started to blaze?

Bienvendios a CVS. Si cuenta con tu Extra Care Card please escanea it now.

There really wasn't money anymore or at least there wasn't money for us.

The man with the camera kissed me and took photographs of the blood that dripped from my fingers.

Everyone knew he was CIA.

He knew for example that the blood that dripped from my face tasted like the blood of the workers assassinated by the Fatherland.

Then I found a dying shack and I met a man with a chain and he was snoring and talking in his sleep and he smelled like pee and complained he had lost his pension when they privatized the city in the dying days of the rotten carcass economy.

Looking after the world is a shitty job if you're really not a people-person.

He slept on the floor with a chain tied to him.

It rode over his crotch and for twenty-three dollars he would bless you into heaven so you would not have to remain in the purgatory of the blazing city.

The further I fall the smaller I become, he chanted.

This poem would be better if it took place in The Saloon of Good Fortune. It would be better if a man jumped off the bar and onto my back as I was reciting it. If I caught him on my back and smashed him into a table. If one of his hoodlum buddies smashed me over the head with a bottle of tequila. This poem would be better with just the right amount of sex, alcohol, violence and 1950s border-noir.

The chained man was moaning about how he had gone from office to office to see what the Good Lord had to offer.

And all I have now, he sang, is a chain and a basket full of fingernails.

An old brown dog was tied by another chain to a rafter.

The dog wouldn't stop yapping and I understood I was being refused absolution.

But I'm Jewish, I told the dog. I am a member of la raza de Moises.

He barks love, the chained man sang, and he wouldn't stop singing and I needed to rest so I would be able to find the boat that would help me get away.

I sat on the floor to sleep, woke up in chains and there was no one to tell my story to.

I lay stiff, holding my breath, trying to be anyone but myself.

Imagination challenge #1:

Imagine there is a matzah-ball bandito in your house. You buy lots of matzah balls and mix them with jalapenos and Fritos and light them on fire and then you survive the apocalypse because Fritos can stay lit forever and you don't need to find kindling or any of that other stuff so you finally have time to study Karlito Marx while watching Manchester United's Mexican hero Chicharito Hernandez score a poacher's golazo in the waning seconds of the Carling Cup while eating hallucinogenic mushrooms while watching Eric Estrada on *Chips* on another screen and listening to a podcast of the Book of Leviticus on your iPod Touch while Skyping with your mom while sexting with your boyfriend who works for the secret police.

Write a sonnet or a villanelle about this experience and do not use any adjectives.

Then I clutched a man trapped beneath my body.

He refused to stop breathing and so did I.

It was 98 degrees.

There were echoes trapped in the wall and they belonged to the broken bodies waiting for the boat on the river.

And the man in my arms said: Are they ordinary people, these trapped voices?

They are ordinary, I said. Demolished, relentless, alone.

And we sang:

Once I made $60,057 a year working for the city. This was before it blazed.

But then one day I came to work and there was an incinerator outside of the building.

My colleagues were scuttling around, trying to salvage things from their offices.

I told this to my boy and all he could say is what, daddy, is an incinerator?

A container for burning refuse, I answered, as they incinerated my desk and a photograph of you that I loved.

I saw them putting my plants and books in it and there was no explanation why.

There was only an automated voicemail on my cell phone from the incinerating bodies who said they were serving the city and that soon all of the city would blaze.

I dream of a giant parasite to feed on the infested bones of the rotting citizens.

There are sirens that won't stop blaring and rotten teeth in all of our mouths and when I asked an authoritative body what to do now that my life had been incinerated he told me to go to the river and ask to be put on a boat.

I went to the river and found a body builder who would not stop running.

He was enormous, wearing only boxer trunks, and he complained that his lover was overusing the word "cock."

He was frantically running and he couldn't stop running and I was looking for the boat and the body builder was screaming about his lover's overuse of the word "cock" and for a moment he spoke of a Jewish centaur on the bank of the river and he kept running and he wouldn't stop running and his boxing trunks were red and silky and when I asked why he was running he shouted that his life was a symbol for something that doesn't exist.

It was 98 degrees.

The evening star came out.

A limp, stale moon hung over us.

And this is where the story should end.

But bedtime stories for the end of the world don't end where they are supposed to end.

They end awkwardly, in the middle of some mess that was probably not worth making to begin with.

Here's an alternative ending.

Imagination Challenge #2:

It's nighttime. You're decomposing in a cage or a cell. Your father is reading the testimonies of the tortured villagers to you. He is in the middle of a particularly poignant passage about how the military tied up the narrator and made him watch as his children were lit on fire. He has to listen to the screams of his blazing children but he cannot listen to their screams so he himself starts screaming and then the soldiers shove a gag in his mouth so that he will stop screaming, but he doesn't stop screaming even with the gag in his mouth.

But these are not screams, actually. They are unclassifiable noises that can only be understood as a collaboration between his dying body, the obliterated earth, and the bodies of those already dead.

Write a free-verse poem about the experience. Write it in the second person.

Publish it some place good.

THE GROSS AND BORDERLESS BODY

This experiment in light poetry continues with an immigrant at the border that separates Indiana from Illinois

It's a dream I have at least a few times a week

The immigrant is a racially ambiguous stateless poet from a country whose name for unitedstatesians is hard to pronounce

The dream-immigrant approaches a very short man who is guarding the border and they have what from a literary perspective is an interesting discussion about the aesthetics of the current reigning Earth God and his relationship to the body of the displaced immigrants roaming the border-territory between Illinois and Indiana

Let's try that again:

Hello, my name is _____

I come from a village where there is no clean water and where if your nose is shaped a certain way, or if you are too tall, or too short, you are likely to be murdered, raped, or dismembered

These tribal feuds date back to the 14th century when a short guy with a long nose slept with the wife of a tall guy with a small nose

Since then, our peoples have hated each other and many of us are in the diaspora

This is not an academic problem

And I don't mean to suggest that there is any 'lightness' to my situation

It totally fucking sucks to have to travel the world, to leave my people and village, and to get stuck in some shit town in Indiana where the portions at the restaurants I can't afford to eat in, except when I am taken to lunch by a minister or a social worker or a rabbi, could provide multiple meals for like eight of my nephews and nieces

I am not used to eating so many potatoes in the morning

Why would anyone eat potatoes in the morning

Here is my body   I could really use a job   Here is my body   I could really use a job   Here is my body   I could really use a job

This experiment in light poetry continues with the immigrant at the border being hacked to death by a so-called early American guarding the sand dunes and the power plants

Or:

He is put to work in the basement of a chemical storage facility that has recently flooded and is filled with excrement, nuclear waste, and the carcasses of washed-up animals

He finishes sucking up the water from the floor

The state keeps flooding and the sewage gets no better and he spends the summer cleaning the excrement off the floor until his body itself is filled with excrement, nuclear waste, and the carcasses of washed up animals

Other nights I dream of a beautiful scoop of ice cream, vanilla bean with hints of mint and jasmine, in a silver dish on a terrace overlooking a war-torn paradise whose citizens are mending their bodies in the aftermath of a Socialist revolution

We are sharing the resources, says a loudspeaker

Now stop eating that ice cream

You are stealing milk that belongs to our children

You should be more conscious of the resources that belong to our children

You are wearing a t-shirt that was made in a factory in a part of the world that smells just like ours

Do you know the people who made your t-shirt

Have you explored your relationship to the people who made your t-shirt

You should tell the store where you bought your t-shirt that they need to charge more money for your t-shirt

They need to charge more money for your t-shirt so that the workers in the factory in the nameless island where your t-shirt is made can afford to buy milk for their children

I call my mom

Mom, is there anyone you know who sews t-shirts

But if I don't buy the t-shirts then isn't this just as bad for the people in the factories

Oh you and your naïve politics

Tell me about that dream again where you are buried amid a pile of corpses in the desert your city has become after its tallest buildings were obliterated by foreigners with missile launchers

Did you hear the one about the tongue that couldn't stop licking everything it saw

It belonged to a unitedstatesian worker whose face was reduced when his union job at the Hyatt Hotel disappeared in the dying days of the rotten carcass economy

This poem is dedicated to that tongue

It's hungry

And thirsty

It will lick every crack on your skin

DREAM SONG #17

They took my body to the forest
They asked me to climb a ladder

I did not want to climb a ladder
But they forced me to climb the ladder

If you don't climb the ladder
we will bury you in the mud

I had to decide   should I die
by hanging   or by burial

I climbed the ladder and they wrapped
a belt around the thick limb of a tree

And when I could no longer breathe
they tossed me into a stream

And I floated to the edge of the village
where someone prayed for my soul

It's like this in a lullaby
for the end of the world:

The options for the end
are endless

But this is not really a lullaby
for the end of the world

It's about the beginning
what happens when we start to rot

in the daylight
The way the light shines on

the ants and worms and parasites
loving our bodies

It's about the swarms of dogs
gnawing our skin and bones

Do you know what it's like
when a ghost licks your intestines

To avoid the hole
the children must sing sweetly, softly

To avoid the hole
they must fill their songs with love

THE PRIVATE WORLD

Did you hear the one about the man they found torched in a garbage can

The police shoved a gas-soaked gag in his mouth and lit a match

The psychiatrists came quickly to council the police officers who were required to set the body on fire

They fed them the appropriate medications, soothed them with the appropriate words, taught them the proper techniques to heal themselves so that they might be able to survive their minds in the murmurs of the rotten carcass economy

Hello. What talks to you at night?

Are you haunted by the voices of the immigrants who suffocated in a truck abandoned on the side of the Arizona highway?

The driver locked them in the back and went off to have a few drinks at the Bar of Good Fortune in Maricopa County

He didn't mean to be gone for sixteen hours

He didn't mean to drink so much he passed out and left them in a truck with no air or water

Oh well

Only a couple died

Ugly people

Actually, he said, I prefer my nightmares with a more urban twist

Meet E

He was shot 7 times at the bus stop last month

Stupid hair

It looked like all the other hair and the shooter thought it was J's hair

They shot him 7 times

Did you hear the one about the refugees who could make the bus stop explode?

The refugees were waiting at the bus stop for the bus to transport them from one detention center to another

They were from New Orleans

They were from Mexico

They were from Rwanda, Iraq, Eritrea, Chicago, Detroit, Sudan, Guatemala, El Salvador, Cuba, Kazakhstan, Syria, etc...

They were from my neighborhood and when they came to your neighborhood their bodies appeared as fields of wheat in flames

A trick of the camera and now they are collapsing bridges that toss foreign cars into an angry, salty ocean

They brought the refugees to the morgue and asked them to imagine their faces on the bodies of birds

It was a gesture developed in a think tank

Their deaths will be easier if they can fly off in a certain direction

The dying man had two bodies

One body was bound for the private world

The other body was bound for another private world

A mouth said: There is only this world

A belly said: They have privatized the forest, the clouds, the sky, the rocks, the water, the trees, the bees, the flowers, the moon

A mouth said: The workers must defend against the privatization of everything

It spat bricks and when the bricks crashed against the sidewalk some little bodies fell out of them

They were replicas of the bodies killed when the coal mine collapsed in West Virginia, China, Colombia, Chile, South Africa, Utah, Bosnia, etc...

Their lungs were black and when you touched their coal-stained faces their skin disappeared

Revolutionary violence disgusts me, the voice said

A voice said: My bones were torn apart first by the police and then by the revolutionaries

They were struggling to solve the same question:

What does it mean to give up your body for an abstraction?

We dragged our bodies to the bank

We sang to the bankers: We feel the need to blame someone for our collective misery

The bankers sang: We are your brothers

Take these bones and suck on them

Take these cubes of ice and rub each other cold as you make love in this horrible vacuum

Brothers, it's okay to set yourselves on fire, to mutilate your bodies in order to protest what you don't understand

Do you want to know a secret?

There is a machine in my mouth that spits and eats and spits and eats and spits and spits and eats

Cadavers, chickens, olives, Easter eggs, bones, blood, words, sand, teeth, children, mountains, deserts, leaves, ghosts, sewers, rivers, mouths, humiliations, calloused hands, sperm, bubbles, wind, blood, rain

The machine wants to do something to your body

It wants to exterminate its empire

It wants to melt your body to bleach your body to fry your body to hold your body to redden your body to freeze your body to lick your body to know your body to explode your body to birth your body to make you vomit and twist into a night cursed with shame and fear

Sorry, sing the bankers to the proletariat, you don't really exist right now

A glitch in the system

Nothing that can't be fixed

By a full-scale overhaul

Of absolutely everything

DREAM SONG #423

Then I stepped out of the sea and into a bonfire on the beach

And the beach became a prairie and the prairie began to reproduce itself

For miles and miles we walked along the fence until we reached an abandoned factory where the workers had all died from dehydration when the manager told them they could no longer afford to have water

Too much time tomando agua, compadré, equal not enough time making t-shirts

Not enough time making t-shirts, Shlomito, equal not enough money to pay you, cabróncito

Not enough money to pay you equal the sidewalk, the park bench, the coyotes banging your head against the side of the trunk

Don't need my intestines, jefecito

Don't need my feet, patroncito

Don't need ojos cara pelo none of that shit they don't let you torture at the United Nations

These were the final words of the borderless body as it crumbled into the sand

I don't remember how the song ends

I think there was a landscape and we put a curtain over it and the children came running out when we pulled up the curtain and they jumped into mountain #423

And they looked for their mothers and fathers but all they found were sheep and goats and lepers

In the last verse we sang a song about the Statue of Liberty, the fastest woman in all of Mexico

I love her, sing the generals and the CEOs

I love her, sing the Bolivians and the Peruvians

I love her sing the beggars and the bankers

I love her rusted body sing the pornographers and the doctors

I love her reverie, her darkness, her malleability, sing the professors

I love her, sings the poet, because she reminds me of my mother and my mother reminds me of myself and I remind myself of my father and all the mouths he needs to feed

I hate living   I do nothing

I love deserts and cacti and the infinite tunnels where my dreamsong turns into a bloodsong splattered from a mouth into a puddle of exploding ventricles, pussed-up pasaportes and hypnotized halos of light

MEMORIES OF MY OVERDEVELOPMENT

There was a time when I wore a suit and tie to pick my mother up at the airport

We waited near the runway and waved at the planes as they took off into the sky

We lived in the tropics but we wore fur hats and wool suits and on the bus the ladies looked glamorous as they wrapped their heads in scarves like Jackie Kennedy

Let me show you everything in my room: here is a cage with two tweeting birds, here is a vanity table, a bed with my various white shirts and dark coats stretched across it

I look out the window and into the sea and compose a suicide note on my typewriter

I need more time to write a shorter suicide note

Instead I write everything, blame everyone from my father to my wife to my sixth grade soccer coach who cut me from the team to Mr. Valtzer my seventh grade teacher who picked me up by my tie and shoved me against the wall to Mr. Baylin the English teacher who used to stick his hands in my pants to tuck my shirt in and his fingers would linger far too long on my ass to Benny who I accidentally knocked over in the 9th grade and who got a concussion and who could not speak for six weeks to the therapist who told me that I was afraid of every emotion in the universe to the girl who broke my heart in college because I was too stupid to understand I was not supposed to call her the day after she kissed me or the next day or the next day and to the doctor who nearly operated on my penis in order to fulfill his monthly quota of operations

I take a break from my suicide note and drink coffee and smoke a cigarette and eat hard tasteless bread with butter in my undershirt

I step out onto the balcony and look through my binoculars and the city looks like the same thing every day

It's a city of cardboard and everyone inside of it wants to float until they land in the wastewater treatment plant of a new nation, some other dream inside of some other body

The bodega stayed the same and the skyline stayed the same and the sea stayed the same and my relationship to the void stayed always and impossibly the same while I kept moving from one world to another

Who was the beast I plucked from the cage

Who was the beast I dropped over the balcony and onto the sidewalk as I yawned and thought about all the disasters occurring inside my body

There is a wound moving, an original wound, moving slowly through my body (tell me more about this, doctor)

Oh I like to see you struggle: between decadence and virility, between virility and femininity, between masculinity and clairvoyance, between godlessness and transparency

I don't know how to measure this:

I have run out of all my imperialist shampoos

I only pay $6 for my shampoo when I used to pay $60

I look vulgar lately

I wear my wife's lipstick as I put on my white shirt and tie and slick back my hair in the style of every other man in every other city in every other office in every other corner of this stupid fucking world

Natural beauty, I write on the mirror with the lipstick, is not nearly as good as artificial beauty

I slip on your pantyhose, love, I slip on your panties, I wear your lipstick as I put on my white shirt and grey tie and set out to destroy myself once more in this city that is like a staircase that winds up my body, a staircase that starts in my toes and slips up my leg and through my groin and through my intestines and up my neck and I vomit it out into the cage where you lock me up when you need to use me for the replaceable services I provide

Oh it feels so cool to stick these pantyhose over my face. Is this the right word, pantyhose?

I don't know the right words for the things you put on your body

I slip your pantyhose over my face and stare at myself in the mirror, at my contorted nose and I am like the Golem of Prague only I live in the tropics which are in the middle of a crumbling Midwestern city where I will be buried under a mountain of ice

I have nothing to do except look into the eyes of people who do not love me

I have nothing to do I want to suffocate myself in the most painless way possible

Since they burned down the department stores, Chicago looks like an atrophied little village in a province

Love and loneliness fill you with different types of illusions

Loneliness fills you with the desire for people to tell you how to live your life

Love, on the other hand, fills you with the desire for everyone to see you living your life

We went to the store to buy coffee and there were so many types of coffee I wanted to beat the crap out of the guy who insisted I hear the story of every type of coffee, where it was roasted, how it was roasted, was it locally roasted or was it roasted in Italy, what flavors was it infused with, so many stupid fucking questions about the coffee that it was almost impossible to believe that just a few days before I had been in a city where there was no coffee

They had run out of coffee

No one knew when they would get more coffee

18,000 children die every day because of hunger and malnutrition and 850 million people go to bed every night with empty stomachs

(How does that make you feel, compadre)

Here we eat flesh we splash around in buckets of milk we slurp up intestines we salivate over raw meat encased in the tubing of a sausage

Sometimes we laugh when we see them starving in their cages and sometimes we bring them little nibs of salamis and sometimes we bring them the horrendous crackers you wanted me to have a whole bag of the first day I visited your city

I doused them in jam so as to forget that this was your life: a bag of tasteless crackers you were actually excited about

You had a starving child in your arms

His chin sunk into your chest and he begged your body to shake him out of his flesh so he could move more swiftly from deathfulness to lifefulness

But at least my hands are clean

I doused them with hand sanitizer

The hand sanitizer was in an enormous container in the waiting room of my therapist's office

My therapist assured me it is not my responsibility that my neighbors are suffering

To be alive is a spiritual mission in which you must get from birth to death without killing yourself

It's not my fault that you are sick and you are dying because I am also sick and I am also dying

It's just that my death is preventable and yours is inevitable

And unlike you my ignorance keeps me from being implicated in the system in which I am involucrated

I could list all the ways I might possibly die but it would be more useful to spend the time telling you that it is not my fault that your life is so fucking miserable

On the other hand, it is absolutely my fault that my life is so fucking miserable

I touch myself nightly to make sure my organs still work

And there is no one here to make my life feel any less mediocre than it already is

I want to talk, today, about my overdevelopment

But instead I pay someone to wipe the dust from my bookshelves and tables

Every body I look at looks exactly the same as my body

This is what's it like to be a defenseless animal

You die because you have failed to install the necessary equipment in your body

You die because you are a counter-revolutionary stuck in the body of an angel

You live because it's too hard to not survive the torture and the interrogation

First your feet start to live, then your legs starts to live, then your hands and arms and mouth and groin and the whole stinking body decides that it will refuse to die

The wind on your face is brutally absent

You can't get back your body anymore

You have sacrificed it to the gurgles, the murmurs, the mountains of foam and dirt

You are the god of hunger in a cage that grows as you get smaller

Death is a mechanic at Jiffy Lube, Juanita

Death is a sales clerk at Target, little Billy

There's a dead Floridian in your hair, Juanita

There's a dead Nebraskan in your Revloned hair, little Billy

Your Revloned hair, Juanita

Your horsehair wig, Juanita

There are 400 mutilated bodies that destroy my sleep, little Billy

It's bedtime, little Billy

It's Clonazepam time, Juanita

It's time, Little Billy, to drink the warm purple milk they sell at Target

We drink it with our Xanax, Juanita

We drink it with our absinthe, Juanita

We drink it with our Wellbutrin, Juanita

We drink and drink, Juanita

We drink it with our Trazodone and Seroquel, Juanita

The sales clerk from Target pisses all over our purple bodies

She digs a hole in the aisle where they sell linens

She takes a belt from the men's wear section and ties it around my neck

Enrich my body with uranium, Juanita

Enrich my body with purple milk, little Billy

Death is a salesclerk from Target, Juanita

She swallows us in the fruit of the vine

She buries us on time

Frogs fly out of her mouth, Juanita

It won't end, Juanita

This poem won't ever end, Juanita

Your psoriasis-covered skin, Juanita

The worms in your ugly mouth, little Billy

The mouth in your ugly mouth, Juanita

The mouth in the mouth of your mouth, little Billy

The mouth in the mouth in the mouth in the mouth in the mouth in the mouth in the mouth in the mouth in the mouth in the mouth of your rotten, carcass mouth, Juanita

EAT NOTHING

It was a tube and clear and plastic and they shoved it into the nose or the stomach or the bowel

Or they placed it directly into the skin and there was a bright light overhead

A card read: Pretend he has an eating disorder

Another card read: Pretend she has dementia

I don't like to put things in my mouth when you talk to me this way

But if you insist on shoving things in my nostrils

Then I will have to tell you what it is like inside my esophagus

Because my smooth muscles contract, things can slide nicely through my intestines

The device in my body passes through the posterior mediastinum in my thorax and enters my abdomen through a hole in my diaphragm at the level of the tenth thoracic vertebra

A voice says: Would you like a wooden gag or a steel gag?

Do you prefer brandy, milk, or cabbage?

I smile because I know how important body language is in front of a TV audience

There are forty-seven women strapped to chairs that recline when a button is pushed

There are fingers in rubber gloves

They squeeze open lips and sing a song about gastric obstructions and psychiatric disorders diagnosed against a lady's consent

When your bowels open, my love, when you think too much about the pharynx: this makes me feel so alone

You know: you always have an alternative means of exercising your right to expression

Vomit is one option   starvation is another

My love, says the authoritative body on the screen

I have a compelling interest in the weight of your frame

How many bureaucrats do we need to affirm this?

Look, love, often people don't really know what they want

They can see an end, but it's not the right end

This is a song about what it feels like when you touch me this way

This is a song about a certain type of fiscal strategy

If they say you can stick things in his body that he doesn't want in his body then you must not say we cannot stick things in his body because there are just too many people who love him

My love, says the authoritative body, you must realize that if I slice off your hand in an act of ungovernable aggression it doesn't mean I don't love you

It all depends on what you need me to say

THE PRIVATIZED WATERS OF DAWN

The appraisers from the Chicago Police Department prod my body in the bathtub

They can't stop coughing in my face

They want to know what street I come from

What code I speak

Who I bought my hair and skin from

What disease I hide in my veins

There are holes in my arm and the appraisers put their cigarettes in them

They don't smoke their cigarettes

They just jam them into my arm

I have a faint idea of what it means to be alive

But almost all of my feelings have been extinguished

I feel my hand at the end of my arm

It is weightless

There are eyes floating in the air and the river won't stop exploding

Earlier, when I was sleeping in the bathtub, I looked up at the ceiling

The little hole of a window exposed a sky the color of blood

I cried into the water and I thought about a note I needed to send to my parents

I needed to tell them my key was with a neighbor

I needed to tell them the four-digit code to my bank account

I needed to tell them that if I died in the water, if I died in the warehouse, if I died in the mud, if I died at the hands of the appraisers, there were some things I needed them to do

The city has disappeared into the privatized cellar of humanity

My street was obliterated from a love that could not be contained by mathematics or emotion

I could not sleep the night before my appointment to be deposited into the private sector

I stared out my bedroom window at 3 AM on a night I could not sleep

I was startled by a police siren

And from my window I watched the police pull a young man out of a black sedan

The driver had long hair

He was gangly and underfed and they asked him to a walk a straight line

You could see hunger in his jawbones

He walked the line perfectly

They put a light to his eye

Follow the light with your eyes, the officer said

They made him stand on one leg

They made him walk on one leg

He walked perfectly on one leg

He stood perfectly on one leg

They made him do twenty pushups

Why do I have to do twenty pushups, he asked

Because you're a decrepit, public body, the police officer said, and you do not own yourself anymore

And the starving driver did the twenty pushups as gracefully as he could

I hid behind the blinds and I wanted to send a signal to the man who was being made to exert himself, to let him know that from here on out every institution he enters is going to be harsh, austere, inflexible

I went back to bed knowing they would put him in the privatized jail cell where he would wake up shrouded in a horrible halo of light

I went back to my bed and a voice kept shouting:

Do you speak English? Do you eat meat? Do you rub meat on your body? Do you own your own body? Do you like to eat raw organ with me? Do you like your organ maggoty? Do you want to know how you can get to the other side of the river?

The voice did not have a body

But it had a mouth

It was the biggest mouth I had ever seen

It opened its mouth and there were small animals inside of it

A dog with two heads was on its tongue and so was a newborn baby and the baby screamed:

Do you have a job? Do you have transferable skills? Do you understand the implications of your inaction? Would you prefer to be grilled, roasted, or boiled?

I said: Where are your eyes?

The mouth said: Your city has disappeared, what are you still doing here?

I said: I work for the city. I was responsible for supplying the youth with degrees of economic value

But this was another life

This was another story

Now I squirm with the other bodies and together we sleep and squirm in the giant bathtubs they cage us in and we do not belong to ourselves

When we are dry we swap bits of clothing, wrinkled up rags, and we warm ourselves in towels filled with our partners' sweat and dirt

The bureaucrats laugh at us when we talk to them

They slurp down raw oysters when we talk to them

They sink their feet into our mouths when we talk to them

They say: Poet your favorite poet from now on is my boot

The poet-boot kicks one of my teeth and I feel it fall into my mouth

I swallow my tooth and wash it down with the bath water I've been sleeping in for the last few days

And when day inevitably breaks I watch the morning ritual:

They take away the horizon

They take away the sky and the streets

They take away the sewers and the beaches and the river and the trees and the birds and the cats and the raccoons and the garbage

And as usual I watch from the bathtub of dawn until someone one comes to conduct the daily appraisal of my body

I cost much less than my historical value and the bank has no choice but to deny the loan I need in order to buy myself back

My deflationary wounds

My privatized blood

My rotten carcass sinking into the privatized waters of dawn

ARCHIVE

(for Valerie Mejer)

We say that absence is a country

We say that in this country the mouth and the lips rent the present tense to the humans who rummage through the garbage in the bodies of the ghosts: the brothers who carry syrup and blood in their cheeks   the crazed deer   a thick, grey liquid escapes through their teeth   the love we look for what a shame to not be able to touch the soul in its hair in its cadaver in the central orifice of its iris

And the ghosts rise from the wet grass into a blood-filled night   a howling night   a night of coronary arteries exploding in a painting in a mouth in a country in a city flooded with garbage and the radiant blood shining forming a layer of paint on the squirrels' fur   the urban skunks   the coyotes calmly walking through the streets of our city that no longer has any public employees

Stranded poets stranded insects abandoned factories

Living here compadre is a death rattle a blow detonating the tongues the teeth the bones of the middle ear the vestibular canals the nerve fibers the tiny hairs....Living in this country is an infection an accumulation of liquid in a cavity eternally producing swelling in the membrane of the ear drum, serous secretion in the external part....

A brief connection between a boy and a porcupine results in a nuclear thesis a mathematical thesis   a calculation of the value of a body plus a country plus all its animals minus all its languages minus the refugees who escape from it minus the rivers minus the lakes minus the trees minus the reduced paisanos plus the hidden owls plus the natural gas plus the artificial blood plus the rain in the forest of your mouth

We say the sky over this country is a liquid dripping from your mouth and the night is a minuscule explosion in your eyes

We say the sky is a night hiding itself in the leaves of the trees covered in the history of our people's violence

In the fever of _____

Today: I look at the images projected from your cheeks

They are memories of my overdevelopment

I am writing a story of love in the time of data fascism

I watch: the ruined sky hanging like a suicide from a tree

A suicide who climbs a bridge and looks down and his eyes fix on the blood that flows from the right ventricle through the pulmonary artery

And the river is crushed to pieces and a kidney rises from the floor of the river

Exhumed intestines spreading across the aridity that's indigenous to our country of thirst

Yes: a sun dissolves   in the face   in the eyes   in the lips of the suicidal sky

And in this book that is a country deposited not in your heart but in your mouth where all your teeth sing as if they were not constantly checking up on the suicidal prisoners

Silence #1

Day #84.39a: the water reappears and rises up to the airplanes that carry bodies and books to the perfect spot for them to fall and fall through an inverted sky

Listen: the sky is screaming at the ash-bodies

And the bodies are little stains in the sky of ash

And these bodies belong to the terrorist group that's called: humanity

A humanity with its map of dust that forms a secret that is a wave that is a tongue sinking into a shoulder   a back where all of the secrets are countries traversed by lungs   by canals   by salt-lagoons trumpeting dawn

And dawn is the border between civilization "X" and civilization "Z"

And on each side of the border they construct tongues covered in sand   in desire   in a sinuous nostalgia

And the tongues lick up the border   they get lost in the glass in the wind in a field sown with wheat with ambassadors of the paths that split me up into unmistakable statistics...

Forced silence #2

Children, listen well: if we would have been tulips (in English)   if we would have been countries burning up on the borders of our ribs

If that's what we would have been then the question you pose would be inevitable

Silence forced from my hope

Calm down, sister...deep breath and don't swallow the seeds of our inexhaustible invisibility

An authoritative voice says: Mama I hope to get to a crumbling country   a historical body that is a cell of a neck of an animal so fragile or so powerful that when it goes out into the sun its cities dissolve   its little jungles dissolve in its mouth

In its granular bones   those fibrous bones   in that nothing silenced by a green poison   malicious   infectious

Unfortunately: I exist

Forced silence #2.2

How can it be that there are people who know nothing of the blows of life

My love is a fragile animal scraping against a whiff of vapor, eating away at the last membrane in your voice   at the crystals shooting out of your face

My love collects invisible stones that are pinholes   that are excavated territories on a beach   on a land that belongs to none of the countries of thirst in your desiccated skin

Your skin filled with parasitic insects

Forced silence #8

I'm old

But I love Blindness #99933

In short: the space where silence is a dawn of blood that really enjoys its exiled existence

Silence #4

The protagonist says: I'd rather not speak

She says: I'd rather walk and walk and not think

She says: The broken light over the buildings makes me want to vomit

(Nature should have more shame)

Forced silence #50

The light that allows us to see *untermenschen* in the letters of a note that can only be written in your skin

Interminable silence #2

Finally and finally and finally

OBLIGED TO PERFORM IN DARKNESS

Let him smack me with the back of his palm
I deserve to be dumped into the sack with the other sick bodies
Run, take my sick body and break it open
The more crushed it gets the easier it will be to see inside of me
You stare at my intestines
My intestines stare back
They are not your friends
You want to tell me something   in the forest you'll find some fingers
They are like berries
They are like the ulcers in my pubic hairs
We are trapped in the cage and they think we will eat mice
But after a few days the mice begin to nibble at our feet
Mother picks a mouse up by its tail
Smacks it against the cage until
Ooze drips from its lips
It shits something out as it drops
She sings a song about eggs

Scrambling, popping in oil, splattering
Mommy who thinks eggs are a delicacy
But my body is contagious
My lips are pussed-up little blisters
Infection crawls up my leg and into my knee
I don't have a knee
I'm a dead man clawing at dead grass in a pop song with a snappy rhythm
Cats paw at my body, kick it around like a rubber toy
When you practice using chopsticks, you practice inside of me
How far do you pull my tongue
There is no water inside my lips
You prove this when you pry them open
I slump by a window in a house in a cage in a forest in a pan full of frying eggs
Checking boxes to indicate my identity
Herniated spleen, check
Crushed ribs, check
Latino, Male, Jewish, Caucasian
Check, check, check, check
This elbow
It is not on my body
It is in your skull, which is in my eyeball
They command you to lick my eyeballs but you are afraid
Throw these bodies parts in a baggie, they sing
Tomorrow you will scoop out some brains
They beat me for scooping out the wrong brains
These are not your brains, they say
The brains to scoop out are your own

THE BROKEN TESTIMONY

There is a beat behind this writing

A nervous tap

Against a plastic-coated table

A body is trying to move forward

It is blocked by its insistence on movement

The performance of stasis played backwards

It disappears or its absence appears

You are writing on my back and I am heaving

You write:

I had a body once but then you made it illegal

Your hard hands inscribe justice into my blank flesh

You write justice into my flesh and I feel something

A clock ticking in the small of my back

I ask you to open the box, to remove the clock

And when you open the box you pull out a ticking clock and say this is your country

It is my nation, I say

And you tell me not to say what I've said before

And I say that I don't *say* anything but I can never stop writing

And you say it was your nation when our bodies were ravaged and you sit me in front of a window

You reproduce me and I watch myself watching a television show with a young couple kissing

This was how I learned to kiss, from studying this scene, and I remember quoting the hands, the eyes, the lips

I want to be like a dumb human, I said, too stupid to be scared

But you are always annoyed to the beat by my insistence on beginning sentences with "but"

And I fall asleep at the window and start dreaming

Which is to say, I start writing

I am writing about a girl I went to school with

She lived up the street from me

She was killed at age 16 by her boyfriend with a sword

Swords in her neck, her back and belly

The boyfriend stabbing himself with the sword

The performance keeps playing itself backwards, and in the present tense

Helicopters circle above the crime scene, searching the woods for the boyfriend

He is stuck in some shrubs

He cannot move his body

He is writing his body into history

He inscribes his body into the trees

With a pistol he shoots himself in the head

There is a constant beat behind this writing

The helicopter lights shine into the thicket

The body of the mutilated girl in the woods

The body of the boy who has blown off his own head

Ravishment and silence and ravishment and word and the writing continues amid the boom of the beat behind us and it is always and inevitably about me

You see:

Today I wrote a novel about a village of cadavers

There was no one left in the village except for one man who witnessed every resident get murdered by the police

Meet Eduardo

He's extremely paranoid

He thinks that at any moment the dead bodies of his neighbors will awaken and stab him in the neck with a machete or an ice pick

He steals their passports and wallets

He lies on top of a dead neighbor and hears a voice inside her

He prefers the word carcass to cadaver

He thinks

I will be thrown into a river to be mauled by by the engines of motorboats

Down, down, into a world of shrieking cadavers who look just like me

Surplus meaning in my nose in my hair in my broken Jewish eyes

I am writing about a mouthful of diseased tongues that won't stop licking each other in deadly ways

I dreamwrite that each tongue in my mouth is a member of the proletariat and they are destroying themselves with their horrible licks

The best dictators don't kill their subjects rather they make their subjects kill each other

I have never fired anyone, says the owner of the plantation

Instead, I have always managed to make the undesirables leave on their own volition

But it *is* fair to ask of a person just what they want from you

And it *is* fair to say that he did not want me until he saw that I was wanted by someone else

And it *is* fair to assume that I did not want myself until I saw that someone else wanted me

And it is neither fair nor unfair that each of our bodies is sinking in the tar to the beat of a traditional song in which the speaker is ravaged as much by love as by its absence

Dead dog barking in the bushes to the beat of this beautiful song

Dead girl screaming in the shrubs to the beat of this beautiful song

Dead writing screaming from the page to the beat of this beautiful song

And you look up at me from the screaming page and I see your face falling from your sunken body

You are jammed into the street in a tar pit on a flaming August day

This is on Montrose Avenue on the North Side of Chicago

Your mutilated body is jammed into a tar pit in the middle of this busy street now empty except for a few scavengers searching for their lost bodies

The helicopter overhead

The creative consultants waiting to turn this misery into poetry

To the beat I stretch out over your tarred-up body

The tar on my clothes forms an inseparable bond between us

You, tarred into the pavement, on your back in the tar, looking up at me

Me, tarred into your body, looking down, to the beat, permanently in your eyes

A glob of tar on your cheek and a glob of tar on my cheek and our faces stick together and the helicopter lights shine down on us

Take us to Kindred Hospital on Montrose Avenue, you say, to the beat of the hovering scavengers a few blocks east of California Avenue

A scavenger has a shovel and I write him into our faces

He takes the shovel and tries to pry apart our faces but they are stuck together and we cannot move and the end of his shovel is caught between my cheek and your cheek

My face {to the beat} relational to your face {to the beat} relational to the tar that holds us together relational to the tar that binds you to the earth

Our silent faces stuck together

Or:

The broken testimony of the broken beat in the broken rhythm of the crumbling excess of my broken mouth and my broken face in the crumbling cadaver of this night

THE DEVOURING ECONOMY OF NATURE

Let's begin at the end, she says.

The best way to end a sentence is with the word "blank."

It is midnight and I am lonely and your blank is the blank of my blank.

He ran through the party that was thrown to celebrate the hanging of the other body; he trampled cold chicken and biscuits.

Or:

He ran through the silhouettes of the hanging bodies.

Or:

He possessed the fortitude needed to refuse to begin another act of language.

I refuse to write the middle of the story.

There is water everywhere.

There is a flood on my street and I am sleeping in a body that is much too big for my bed.

In fact I am sleeping in a bed that is much too big for my house.

The flood has changed the proportions (house>bed>body) or at least my perception of the proportions.

Did you hear the one about the immigrant laborer who was run over by the tractor? In his pocket was a photograph of his cousin Ewa, a 13-year-old in a refugee camp in another country. As the tractor ran him over, he kept shouting to his fellow workers: Please, somebody, marry Ewa. Somebody! Marry! Ewa!

And to mourn the death of the mutilated workers the children sang a song called "Other People's Bodies."

They sang it to the tune of a current popular song.

There was a dance routine that involved hand motions and little hops and the thrusting of booties in and out.

And as the song developed, the progression of data became increasingly relevant, for as the children sang they slowly began to understand that they would never see their parents again, that they had been taken from their homes and tossed into the pools in order to fulfill the required data specifications outlined by the city, the state, and the country.

Or:

A barbarian and an economist walk into a bar.

The barbarian says:

I dreamt we were in a swimming pool and you were swimming towards me. I was sitting on the wall and when you got to the wall the wall dissolved into the water and the pool stretched out endlessly and there were hundreds of children swimming in the pool and they were looking for their parents. There were men in orange wet suits painting lines throughout the water. Over the water, really. And the lines were different colors and they stuck to the surface of the water and we understood that certain colors meant certain things. And you picked up a drowning child and said: Here is a small piece of data. I won't tell you what this data means in relation to the other data that will determine the relationship between your desire to eat the children and the future prosperity of the nation.

The economist orders two martinis and says to the barbarian:

There is something frozen here. I see you standing in front of the pool and I know that the you who is standing there is the you who has uttered this sentence so many times before. When you spit out the sentence they will say that it did not come from your mouth, that it came from the mouth of the person who was performing this act of being you.

In other words, linguistic theory opens the door to the possibility that we are not ethically responsible for our actions.

And the barbarian says:

Even if money doesn't exist, there will always be an audience for economists.

And they take the water from the river and put it in the back of several trucks. And from the dried up river there emerges a country. And in the country there are children who have been invented by people who made money in things that do not actually exist...

And they don't say: Why are you taking the water from the river?

And they don't think: Why are you shaving the fur from the bodies of our dogs?

The children sit on the sofa placed perfectly in a picturesque location on the river. The dogs are arranged so that they rest in front of the sofa. The photographer asks the children to smile so that the rest of the world can see how well we treat the displaced people.

Do you want to see what you look like, the photographer says to the children.

The children look at their images without recognition, stuck as they are in the fantasy life of the economists.

And the barbarian says:

Do we really need these kids? Do I really need this job?

Three dogs guard the two children.

I will write their story but I will not understand it.

The doctor says, Yes, in Illinois we love a war between states, across borders both real and imagined.

Or:

Did you hear the one about the boy who was thrown into the fire?

His charred meat was hacked up with a cleaver and fed to dogs while his parents watched from a cage.

The economist, formerly of the working class, only got married so that he could demonstrate that it was possible for a 'kid like me' to move into high society.

According to the data, it is impossible for rich people to be friends with poor people.

This, according to the data, is true in all societies.

LAKE MICHIGAN MERGES
INTO THE BAY OF VALPARAISO, CHILE

the reasons for which our blood is drawn in the prison camps of Lake Michigan are not communicated to us

the reasons for which we are imprisoned are also not communicated to us

it is often said on the shores of Lake Michigan, which is the Bay of Valparaiso, that we will die for reasons we do not understand

we do not understand why we do not understand why we will die

we do not understand why we do not understand why we are imprisoned

we do not understand why we do not understand why we are paid or beaten or loved

we do not understand why last night the authoritative bodies loaded up four ships worth of prisoners and why those boats are half a mile away from the beach, booming dance music, baking in the summer sun we do not understand why the authoritative bodies don't sweep the carcasses of the dead pets and washed up animals off the beaches on which we walk and sleep

we do not understand our relationship one body to another

at times the authoritative bodies tell us to touch each other

at times they tell us to feed each other

at times they tell us to beat each other

at times they tell us to pay each other

at times they tell us to protect each other

at times they tell us to kiss each other

at times they tell us to probe each other with forceps, needles, and wooden skewers

at times they force us to force each other to drink dirty purple milk and to eat rotten bread and vegetables

at times they tell us to stick juicy oranges into each other's mouths

at times they tell us to kick each other and call each other offensive names

at times they tell us to chew and swallow everything

at times they tell us to curse and laugh and hiss

at times they say: pretend you are an immigrant and hiss for us at times they say: pretend you are not an immigrant and speak as if you are not a communist

or they say: your faces are organs of emotional communication: smile or frown or cry

or they say: pretend you are a machine and that you do not have a soul

or they say: you are nothing more than a piece of data to be aggregated, to be disaggregated, to be sliced and diced into the most minute units so that we can understand how the body and the city and the nation whir and wallow and tick

or they say: you are a human machine and you must explode

there is good money, they say, in emotional responsiveness

and at times they pay us when we laugh or snarl or cry

or they say: there is nothing to be gained from emotional responsiveness

so they beat us when we laugh or snarl or cry

and they say: you have shame in your eyeballs, you have love in our eyeballs, you have pain in your dimples, you have guilt in your mouth, abjection in your lips, joy in your nostrils, anger in your cheekbones, love in the bags under your eyes, passion in your eyebrows, fear in your chin, disgust in your forehead, disaster and promise and despair in the furrows of your face and in the murmuring economies on your rotten carcass tongue

LAKE MICHIGAN, SCENE #X1C290.341AB3DY

1

There is a yellow barrier in front of a warehouse on the west side of Chicago

An authoritative body with a gun wears a leather jacket that says "Policia" on the back of it

There are no secrets

The prisoneres are tortured in a secret police compound that everyone knows about

Hola mira estamos en el centro del mundo no me gusta estar tan conectado a la tierra prefiero viajar por el espacio sideral los planetas las estrellas

el mundo me aburre dice el cuerpo autoritario

me voy a Chicago me voy a Jupiter me a voy Saturno

vamos a Chicago es mucho más fácil que nos maten o que matemos o que liberemos nuestras almas de nuestros cuerpos o vice-fooking-versa

PUNTO

PERIOD

Do you read me?

-Yes, Hi

See it's hard being in the center of the country being in the center of the country it's a bit like being in the center of the universe I'd rather be in outer space moving through planets and stars oh Earth you are so boring not like on Saturn or Jupiter or the moon brothers and sisters and earthlings let us go to Chicago it's so much easier to be killed there or to kill or to free our souls from our bodies I mean our bodies from our souls....

Did you hear the one about the military gang that called the mayor in the middle of the night demanding money to save his daughter?

A girl's voice could be heard on the other end, gagged and muffled

But ha ha ha the mayor knew better: his daughter was not at home, she was vacationing on Lake Geneva on the southern tip of Wisconsin

The criminals were arrested after the location of their cellular phones was detected through sophisticated satellite software

The criminals went to jail where they molded forever and ever

2

The authoritative bodies screen films at night in the prison camps on the beaches at the northern end of Chicago

There's one they project on Sundays on the outer wall of the prison

We sit on the sand and watch it under the mist and moon

The authoritative bodies tell us to laugh and when we don't laugh they beat us

They tell us to cry and when we cry they beat us

They command us to make little sounds to signal that we are experiencing aesthetic or emotional pleasure as we watch the Sunday night film that begins in a warehouse, a holding cell for immigrants who are smuggled across the border

Meet M, the star of the film....she's a mother of 3

Her children are in California

She does not have papers

She has paid a smuggler $6200 to help her cross the border and when she makes it into Arizona her family members will have to pay more money to finish the deal

There she is in a cell crammed wall-to-wall with other people who have paid thousands of dollars and are now stuck in an airless shack until the smugglers decide it's okay to leave

The sun rises and now she is walking through the desert

Overhead shot of barrel cacti, brittlebush, chain fruit cholla, Joshua trees, jumping chollas, Mojave aster, soaptree yucca, prickly pear cacti

Lizards, Gila monsters, bobcats, tortoises, desert toads, pygmy owls, thorny devils

The immigrants in the film are weak, hungry, barely able to move

Some are stumbling to the ground, or crawling, or completely unable to move

But just as you think they are going to collapse from dehydration, together they start to sing:

Ay que bonito es volar, a la 2 de la mañana, a la 2 de la mañana, ay que bonito es volar, ay mama, volar y volar y volar, a la 2 de la mañana, a la 2 de la mañana, ay que bonito es volar ay mama

And there is a miracle

They begin to fly

They begin to fly over the border like witches

They are witches and they fly over the border

And they sing:

It's so beautiful to fly It is soooooo beautiful to fly

And they do not die of dehydration

And they are not arrested

And their smugglers are arrested and forced to return the thousands of dollars they have taken from them

The immigrants fly and fly across the desert until they land in the middle of a cosmopolitan city where a handsome, kind bureaucrat takes them to a hotel where they are given a warm bed and bath for the night; a few hundred dollars to get to their next location; the appropriate documents so that they can work and have health care

They are welcomed by the bureaucrats with gratitude, joy, and compassion

Ay que bonito es volar

And as we watch the film they make us sing on the beaches of Lake Michigan:

It's so beautiful to fly, so beautiful to fly

And we sing as loud as we can so that they can hear us on the prison ships a half mile off the coast

Hay que bonito es volar, a la 2 de la mañana, a la 2 de la mañana, hay que bonito es volar ay mama

And tonight as we watch our brothers and sisters flying across the desert there are no machetes

There is no blood on our bodies

There are no forceps jammed into our orifices

There are no kicks, no blows, no handcuffs

Damn it feels good to fly

It's what the body must always remember

THE MOUNTAIN AT THE END OF THIS BOOK

The politics of the mountain render invisible the paths of dogshit and horseshit and human shit that crisscross the mountain.

To leave the mountain, you need a good reason to not want to be dead.

This mountain appears in every book I have ever written. Sorry if you were expecting something new.

But you are not the city, sing the bodies to the police who bury them.

We live in one of the deadliest cities in the world, a boring observation.

The self in the story is equivalent to the period at the end of this sentence, which is equivalent to the dying bodies who refuse to fall off the top of the mountain.

They dump the bodies at the base of city hall and the administrators from the Board of Education dig through their dead pockets and steal coins, identification cards, pencils, notebooks, and blood.

And they drill the body of a sunken child into the side of the wooden mountain.

And they take a fallen bird and nail it to the wooden wall they have drilled into the body of a sunken child.

Their hands are covered in the milk they dump on us as we starve.

A helicopter overhead dumps thousands of loaves of bread so crushed up we can hardly eat them.

Last night on the mountain at 1:41 AM body A shot body B then body C shot body B and bodies D and E dumped the bodies of A and B and C at the foot of the mountain then 350,000 displaced children came to sing them songs of beauty, glory, and love.

There is a beat that runs through the mountain and the boarded-up walls of the broken building where they sent us when we were wards of the state and they loved us.

Feel the barbed wires slicing into our bodies.

This mountain is the last breath of this bedtime story for the end of the world.

And the bureaucrats allocate $643,000 so that in the next narrative we will become other than what we are, other than what we think we are, other than what they think we are, other than what they know us to be.

We want you to become other than what you are, chant the bureaucrats.

Imagine you are not what you are!

We are convinced that you will be most like yourselves when you become other than what you are, chant the bureaucrats.

And they pay us and they love us and they beat us.

And they pay us and they love us and they beat us until we stop climbing this insufferable mountain.

The mountain is collapsing.

Feel the mountain closing in on us.

Feel the mud of the mountain enveloping us.

Feel our bodies disappearing into the mud of the mountain.

Feel the mud filling our mouths with sludge and worms and bubbling foam.

Feel the mountain destroying the bodies that loved it.

Stop and feel the nothing you now stand in.

Stop and feel the absence of this sentence.

Stop, now, in the middle of this sentence and pretend it's not here.

It's not here.

You're not here.

You're in the middle of another mountain, the middle of another narrative, the middle of another love, the middle of another sentence.

And you say: I will love you, and never again.

And I say: I will love you, and never again.

We do not know how to read the mountain without love yet we transpose a city on top of it and fill it with our dreams and fears.

Children with florescent lights in their bodies, children with worms in their mouths and ears sink into the tar pits on the mountain in this bedtime story for the end of the world.

There are body bags and 350,000 children in the streets leading up to this mountain.

I hear the suffocated cries of a falling body sinking into the middle of the street and shouting: This is not my city, these are not my streets. This is not my mountain.

The bodies of the neighborhood children are collected and tossed onto the base of the mountain that has emerged out of the sinking flatness.

Ramon, Marcus, Sammy, David, Gilberto (we are with you in your rock lands).

The boys are in the mountain and there is something foaming around them.

There are brick stairs surrounding the mountain and over the bricks are barbed wires and over the barbed wires there is ivy.

The barbed wires are to prevent people from climbing onto the mountain to commune with the bodies they love.

Thousands of slain bodies piled at the base of the mountain that the administrators have constructed in order for us to believe in the possibility of our bodies.

Still, this one is personal.

It's about my desire to sleep, forever, in the sinking commune of your rotten carcass mouth.

Mountain, I love how you are an incredible combination of molecules, an indissoluble aggregate of matter, a chain of sonorous bodies bouncing infinitely through tunnels at the bottom of the biggest poem there ever was.

On the mountain, my body looks better when it is filled with other bodies.

And my mouth looks better when it is filled with other mouths.

And the valleys look better when they are filled with other valleys.

On the mountain, the poets lunge and growl and snort and belch.

They spit natural selection poems out of their eyes. Ethnic avant-garde poems drop from their prickly mouths.

On the mountain, the free-market poems absorb themselves and regenerate into billions of the blankest verses there ever were.

A pharmaceutical heiress dies and gives us six million dollars to spend on poetry.

The night sky is enjambed with rotten assets.

The poets on the mountain have barricaded my body and I will spend eternity trying to pry the wood from my flesh.

The abandoned children carve beautiful epitaphs on stolen slabs of meat.

I look down into this mountain of gyrating bodies and sing a peaceful song about austerity and the privatization of our form and content.

At the base of the mountain there are frugal bureaucrat-poets making love in mud houses that float in sewers.

There are abandoned boys in the windows of these houses.

Come find us, they write on the sweaty glass, as they disappear into the bubbling mud.

DANIEL BORZUTZKY's *The Performance of Becoming Human* won the 2016 National Book Award in Poetry. His books and chapbooks include, among others, *In the Murmurs of the Rotten Carcass Economy* (2015), *Bedtime Stories for the End of the World!* (2015), *Data Bodies* (2013), *The Book of Interfering Bodies* (2011), and *The Ecstasy of Capitulation* (2007). He has translated Galo Ghigliotto's *Valdivia* (2016), Raúl Zurita's *The Country of Planks* (2015) and *Song for his Disappeared Love* (2010), and Jaime Luis Huenún's *Port Trakl* (2008). His work has been supported by the Illinois Arts Council, the National Endowment for the Arts, and the Pen/Heim Translation Fund. He lives in Chicago.

All books are available at BrooklynArtsPress.com

Alejandro Ventura, *Puerto Rico*
Alex Green, *Emergency Anthems*
Alexander Boldizar, *The Ugly*
Anaïs Duplan, *Take This Stallion*
Anselm Berrigan & Jonathan Allen, *LOADING*
Bill Rasmovicz, *Idiopaths*
Broc Rossell, *Unpublished Poems*
Carol Guess, *Darling Endangered*
Chris O. Cook, *To Lose & to Pretend*
Christopher Hennessy, *Love-In-Idleness*
Daniel Borzutzky, *The Performance of Becoming Human*
Debora Kuan, *Lunch Portraits*
Dominique Townsend, *The Weather & Our Tempers*
Erika Jo Brown, *I'm Your Huckleberry*
Jackie Clark, *Aphoria*
Jared Harel, *The Body Double*
Jay Besemer, *Chelate*
Jay Besemer, *Telephone*
Joanna Penn Cooper, *The Itinerant Girl's Guide to Self-Hypnosis*
Joe Fletcher, *Already It Is Dusk*
Joe Pan, *Autobiomythography & Gallery*
John F. Buckley & Martin Ott, *Poets' Guide to America*
John F. Buckley & Martin Ott, *Yankee Broadcast Network*
Joseph P. Wood, *Broken Cage*
Julia Cohen, *Collateral Light*
Lauren Russell, *Dream-Clung, Gone*
Laurie Filipelli, *Elseplace*
Martin Rock, *Dear Mark*
Matt Runkle, *The Story of How All Animals Are Equal, & Other Tales*
Matt Shears, *10,000 Wallpapers*
Matt Shears, *Dear Everyone*
Michelle Gil-Montero, *Attached Houses*
Noah Eli Gordon, *The Word* Kingdom *in the Word Kingdom*
Paige Taggart, *Or Replica*
Seth Landman, *Confidence*
Various, *Responsive Listening: Theater Training for Contemporary
    Spaces*, Eds. Camilla Eeg-Tverbakk & Karmenlara Ely
Wendy Xu, *Naturalism*